The Speci   Ride

Story by Stephen Harrison

Illustrations by Genevieve Rees

NELSON PRICE MILBURN

Nick and Abby waved
to their aunt and uncle
as the car stopped at the farmhouse.
"We've brought our bikes, Aunty Kath,"
called Abby.

Nick climbed out of the car.
"Dad told us that you've made a special ride
for us," he said.
"Where are we going, Uncle John?"

"You'll have to wait and see," said his uncle.
"Your dad's going to help me
mend some fences this morning.
Then we'll meet you for lunch
at the back of the farm.
We'll take all the food with us now."

Aunty Kath smiled at the children. "We're going to ride our bikes to the picnic spot," she said.

Later in the morning,
the children set off with Aunty Kath.
"We've made a new bike track," she told them.
"We thought you'd enjoy our special ride.
Part of the track goes through the bush."
She pointed to some trees in the distance.

4

When they reached the track,
they went in single file.
It was cool and shady riding along
under the tall trees.

After a while, they could see sunlight
shining down through the leaves.
The track led them out of the bush
and onto a grassy hillside.

"You can have as many turns as you like
on this flying fox," grinned Uncle John,
as he came up a track towards them.
"Just leave your helmets on.
And we've tied a rope to the pulley
so that you can bring it back up here
after each ride."

"I'll go first so you can see how it's done,"
Nick said to Abby.
"You just have to hang on and go flying down —
it's the greatest ride."

"Here I go!" he yelled.   He lifted his feet,
and sailed all the way down to the grass below.

Then it was Abby's turn.
Nick took the rope
and tugged the pulley up the wire
as he went back up the track.

Uncle John held the pulley
while Abby reached for the handles.

"Come on," called Aunty Kath.
"We'll catch you!"

Abby held on tightly,
and lifted her feet just as Nick had done.
Slowly she began to slide along the wire.
Then away she flew,
down to the picnic spot.

"It **is** the greatest ride," she called.

The children raced back up the track.
Then down they went on the flying fox again,
shouting and laughing as they landed
on the grass.

"I thought you two were hungry,"
said Aunty Kath.

"We are," shouted Abby,
"but we're having too much fun!"

"We're coming to the picnic
on the flying fox!" laughed Nick.